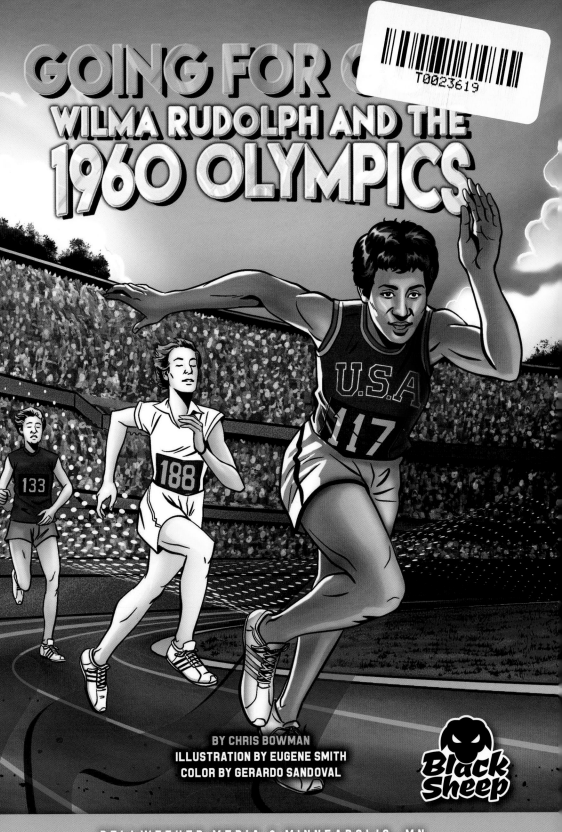

GOING FOR G...
WILMA RUDOLPH AND THE
1960 OLYMPICS

BY CHRIS BOWMAN
ILLUSTRATION BY EUGENE SMITH
COLOR BY GERARDO SANDOVAL

Black Sheep

BELLWETHER MEDIA • MINNEAPOLIS, MN

STRAY FROM REGULAR READS WITH BLACK SHEEP BOOKS. FEEL A RUSH WITH EVERY READ!

This edition first published in 2024 by Bellwether Media, Inc.

No part of this publication may be reproduced in whole or in part without written permission of the publisher. For information regarding permission, write to Bellwether Media, Inc., Attention: Permissions Department, 6012 Blue Circle Drive, Minnetonka, MN 55343.

Library of Congress Cataloging-in-Publication Data

Names: Bowman, Chris, 1990- author. | Smith, Eugene (Illustrator), illustrator.
Title: Going for gold : Wilma Rudolph and the 1960 Olympics / by Chris Bowman ; [illustrated by Eugene Smith].
Description: Minneapolis, MN : Bellwether Media, Inc., 2024. | Series: Black Sheep. Greatest moments in sports | Includes bibliographical references and index. | Audience: Ages 7-13 years | Audience: Grades 4-6 | Summary: "Exciting illustrations follow the events of Wilma Rudolph competing in the 1960 Olympics. The combination of brightly colored panels and leveled text is intended for students in grades 3 through 8"–Provided by publisher.
Identifiers: LCCN 2023017795 (print) | LCCN 2023017796 (ebook) | ISBN 9798886875072 (library binding) | ISBN 9798886875577 (paperback) | ISBN 9798886876956 (ebook)
Subjects: LCSH: Rudolph, Wilma, 1940-1994–Juvenile literature. | Women runners–United States–Biography–Juvenile literature. | Runners (Sports)–United States–Biography–Juvenile literature. | Olympic Games (17th : 1960 : Rome, Italy)
Classification: LCC GV1061.15.R83 B68 2024 (print) | LCC GV1061.15.R83 (ebook) | DDC 796.42092 [B]–dc23/eng/20230513
LC record available at https://lccn.loc.gov/2023017795
LC ebook record available at https://lccn.loc.gov/2023017796

Editor: Betsy Rathburn   Designer: Andrea Schneider

Printed in the United States of America, North Mankato, MN.

TABLE OF CONTENTS

Red text identifies historical quotes.

A TASTE OF GLORY

1956 Summer Olympics. Melbourne, Australia.

American sprinter Wilma Rudolph is competing in her first Olympic Games. She is only 16 years old.

Wilma is running in the first **heat** of the 200-meter dash. If she does well, she will be one step closer to the 200-meter dash finals.

Unfortunately, Wilma does not run fast enough to make the finals.

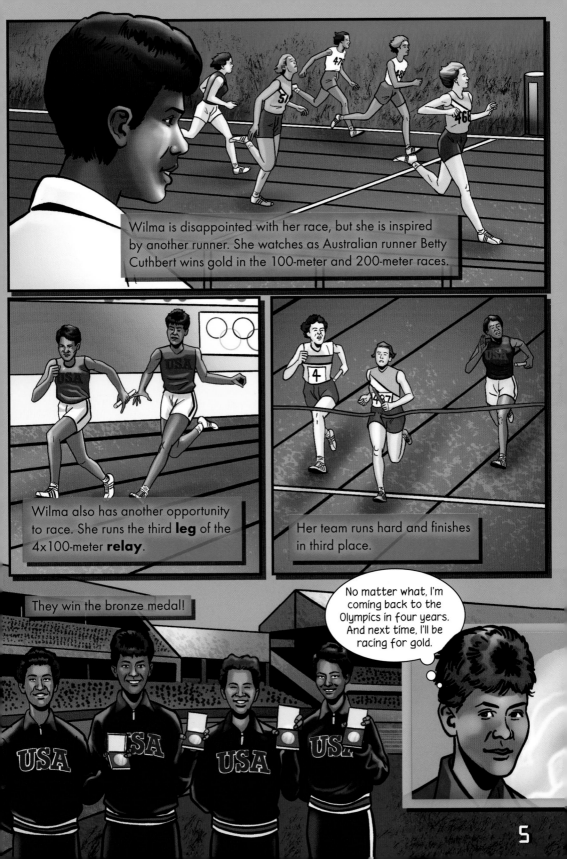

Wilma is disappointed with her race, but she is inspired by another runner. She watches as Australian runner Betty Cuthbert wins gold in the 100-meter and 200-meter races.

Wilma also has another opportunity to race. She runs the third **leg** of the 4x100-meter **relay**.

Her team runs hard and finishes in third place.

They win the bronze medal!

No matter what, I'm coming back to the Olympics in four years. And next time, I'll be racing for gold.

LEARNING TO RUN

As a child, Wilma is often sick. She struggles with **pneumonia** and **scarlet fever**. At a young age, she gets **polio**.

Polio causes Wilma's left leg to be partly **paralyzed**. She has trouble standing and walking.

How long will she need this brace?

She will never be able to walk without it.

Because of her leg, Wilma is not able to go to school. A teacher brings schoolwork to her home. Wilma is often bored and unhappy being inside all day. When she does see other kids, they often tease her about her leg.

It's not going to be like this forever.

At this time, the United States is **segregated**. Black and white people have separate schools, hospitals, and stores. Wilma and her mother must travel to a Black hospital in Nashville for treatment on Wilma's leg. The hospital is far away.

Wilma's mother massages her leg every day to help it heal.

Why do we do this if the doctors say my leg won't heal?

Your leg will heal. It might take time, but you will get stronger.

Ouch!

Wilma regularly tries walking around her house without the brace on. She often falls, but she keeps trying.

In time, Wilma is able to go to school. Her brace helps her move around more easily. She is finally able to play with friends!

Soon, Wilma's brace is replaced with a special shoe. But she wants to improve more. She continues to practice walking without the shoe.

Her hard work makes her leg stronger. By age 12, she no longer needs the brace or special shoe!

But Wilma pays close attention to the games. By 9th grade, she finally starts to get playing time.

Wilma, you're in!

Thanks, coach!

th grade, Wilma goes out for her school's
ketball team. Unfortunately, she does not
o play in a game for two years!

same year, Wilma's coach starts a
k and field team for her school.

Running track should really help us in the basketball season!

Go!

Wilma enjoys track. She's faster than a lot of her teammates, and she works hard to get better. Wilma wins every track race she enters as a 9th grader!

FASTER AND STRONGER

In her fourth year on the basketball team, Wilma gets more playing time. She helps lead her team to the state **tournament**.

One of the referees is Ed Temple. He is also the women's track coach at Tennessee State University.

The next year, Coach Temple invites Wilma to train at his summer camp for track athletes at Tennessee State.

She will practice with other track athletes.

But she's still in high school.

Yes, but if she works hard, she can earn a **scholarship** to Tennessee State!

At first, Coach Temple has his athletes run long distances up to three times a day. This helps make Wilma stronger and build up her **endurance**.

But soon, the athletes run shorter races to work on their speed. Wilma learns how to use starting blocks. These help her begin her races with more power.

Remember to stay relaxed!

Coach Temple enters his runners into a few meets that summer. At one meet in Philadelphia, Pennsylvania, Wilma wins all nine of her races!

After one of her races, Wilma meets legendary baseball players, Jackie Robinson and Don Newcombe.

Keep running, Wilma!

Don't let anything, or anybody, keep you from running.

TENN STATE UNIVERSITY

Wilma is inspired by the meeting. She decides to keep running no matter what.

After a summer of hard work, Wilma is in great shape. Coach Temple asks her to run at the 1956 U.S. **Olympic Trials**. She travels to the event with her fastest teammates.

Wilma enters the 200-meter dash and the 4x100-meter relay with her friend and teammate, Mae Faggs.

You stick with me in the race, you make the team.

Wilma runs hard and keeps up with Mae. They both **qualify** for the 1956 Olympics in Melbourne, Australia!

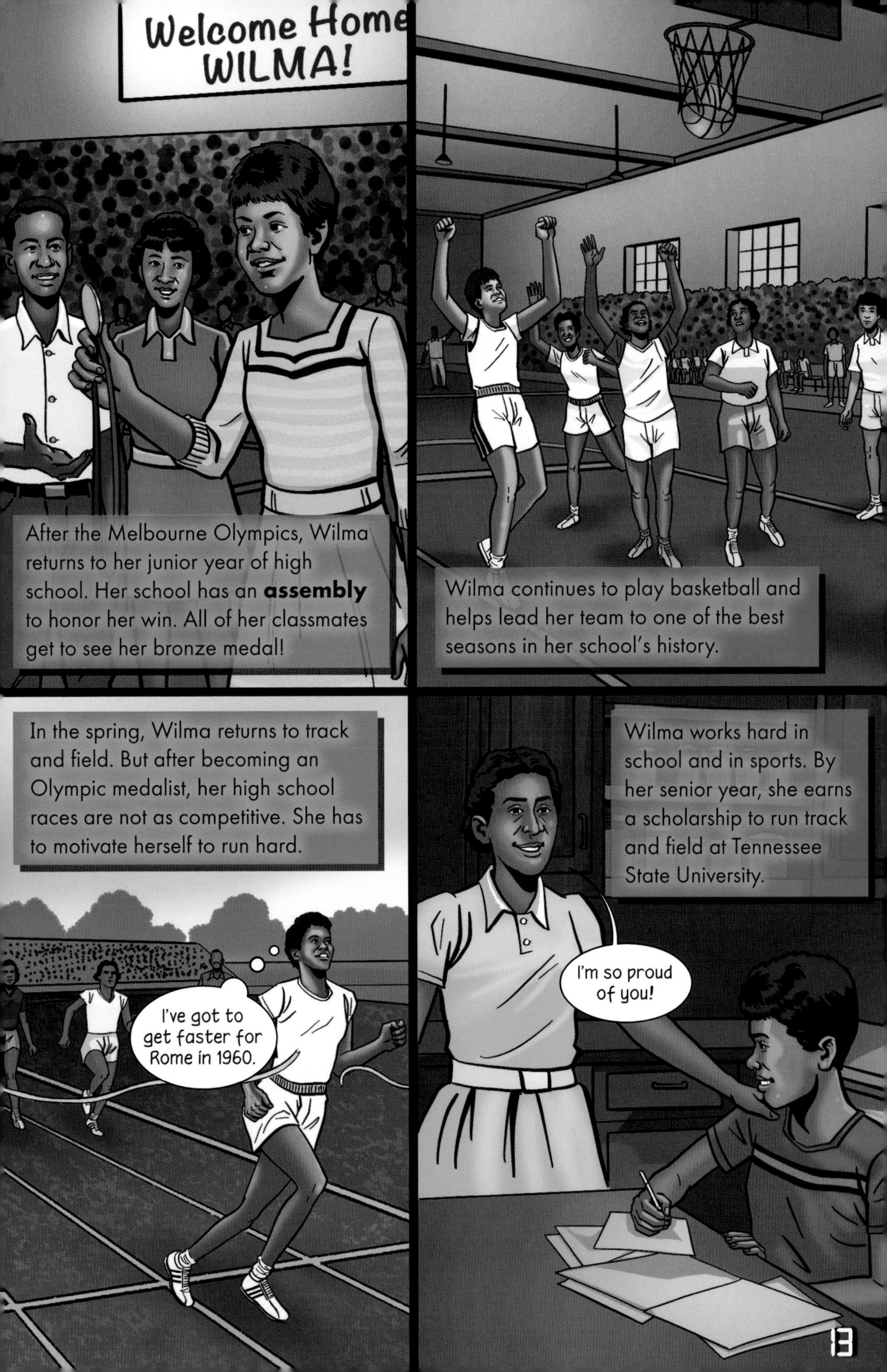
Welcome Home WILMA!
After the Melbourne Olympics, Wilma returns to her junior year of high school. Her school has an **assembly** to honor her win. All of her classmates get to see her bronze medal!
Wilma continues to play basketball and helps lead her team to one of the best seasons in her school's history.
In the spring, Wilma returns to track and field. But after becoming an Olympic medalist, her high school races are not as competitive. She has to motivate herself to run hard.
I've got to get faster for Rome in 1960.
Wilma works hard in school and in sports. By her senior year, she earns a scholarship to run track and field at Tennessee State University.
I'm so proud of you!

Wilma faces challenges before starting college. In the summer of 1958, she and her boyfriend, Robert, have a baby girl. She knows people will judge her for having a baby so young.

Family members agree to care for the baby. Because of this, Wilma can go to college and continue running.

In college, Wilma continues to train as a runner. She and her team travel to Chicago, Illinois, to compete in the 1959 Pan American Games.

Runners from many countries participate. Wilma wins a silver medal in the 100-meter dash.

More success follows. Two days later, Wilma and her team win gold in the 4x100-meter relay!

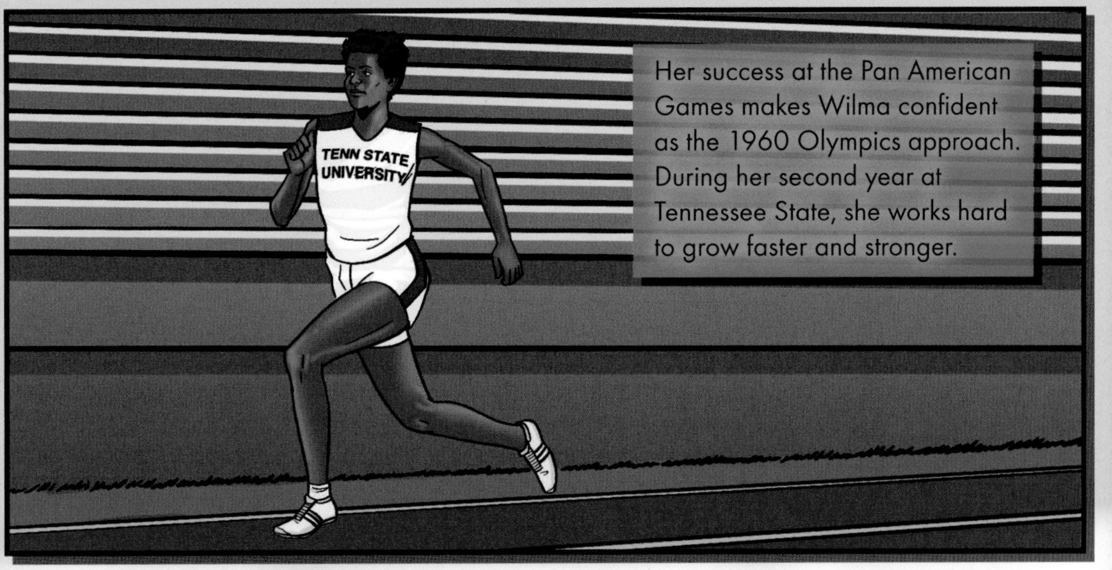
Her success at the Pan American Games makes Wilma confident as the 1960 Olympics approach. During her second year at Tennessee State, she works hard to grow faster and stronger.
TENN STATE UNIVERSITY

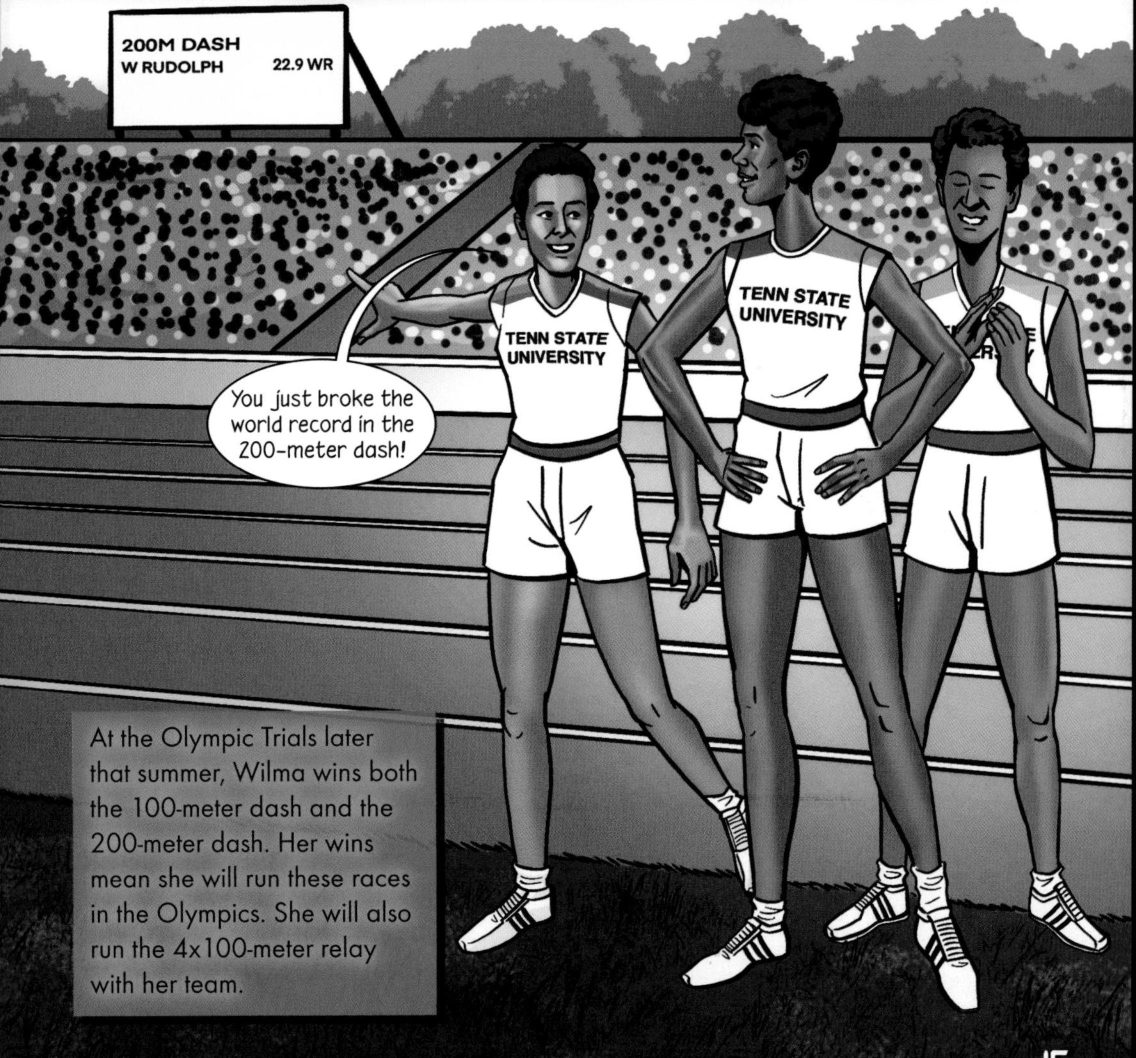
200M DASH
W RUDOLPH 22.9 WR
TENN STATE UNIVERSITY
TENN STATE UNIVERSITY
You just broke the world record in the 200-meter dash!
At the Olympic Trials later that summer, Wilma wins both the 100-meter dash and the 200-meter dash. Her wins mean she will run these races in the Olympics. She will also run the 4x100-meter relay with her team.

GOING FOR GOLD

1960 Summer Olympics. Rome, Italy.

Wilma and the rest of the U.S. team get to the Olympics early to practice before their events begin.

On the day before her first race, Wilma and her teammates cool down after a workout. As they jog around a field, Wilma steps in a hole and hurts her ankle.

Ouch!

She worries she will not be able to run.

The next morning, Wilma is relieved to find that she can walk on her own.

How's your ankle?

It hurts, but I'll give it a shot.

You've trained so hard. You're ready for this.

As Wilma steps out onto the track, she is greeted by the crowd cheering her name. Her fast times leading up to the Olympics have made her a fan favorite.

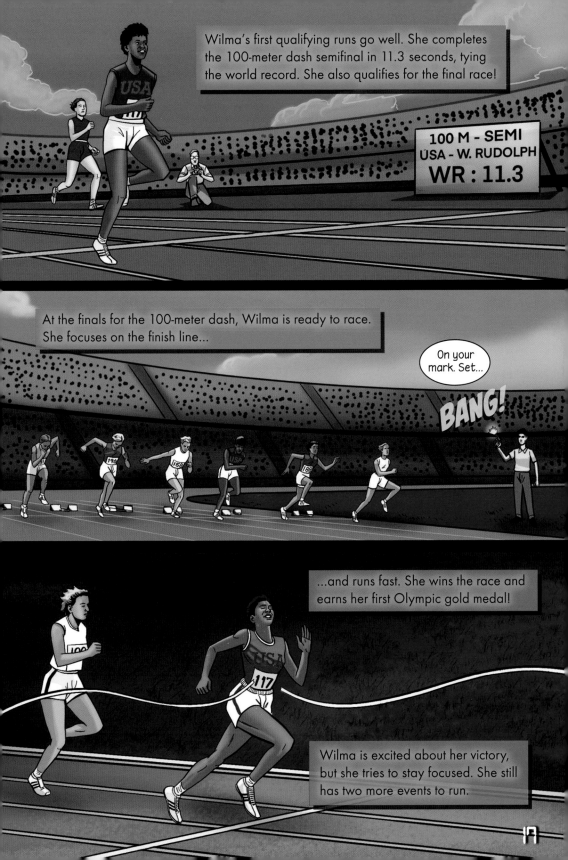

Wilma's first qualifying runs go well. She completes the 100-meter dash semifinal in 11.3 seconds, tying the world record. She also qualifies for the final race!

100 M - SEMI
USA - W. RUDOLPH
WR : 11.3

At the finals for the 100-meter dash, Wilma is ready to race. She focuses on the finish line...

On your mark. Set...

BANG!

...and runs fast. She wins the race and earns her first Olympic gold medal!

Wilma is excited about her victory, but she tries to stay focused. She still has two more events to run.

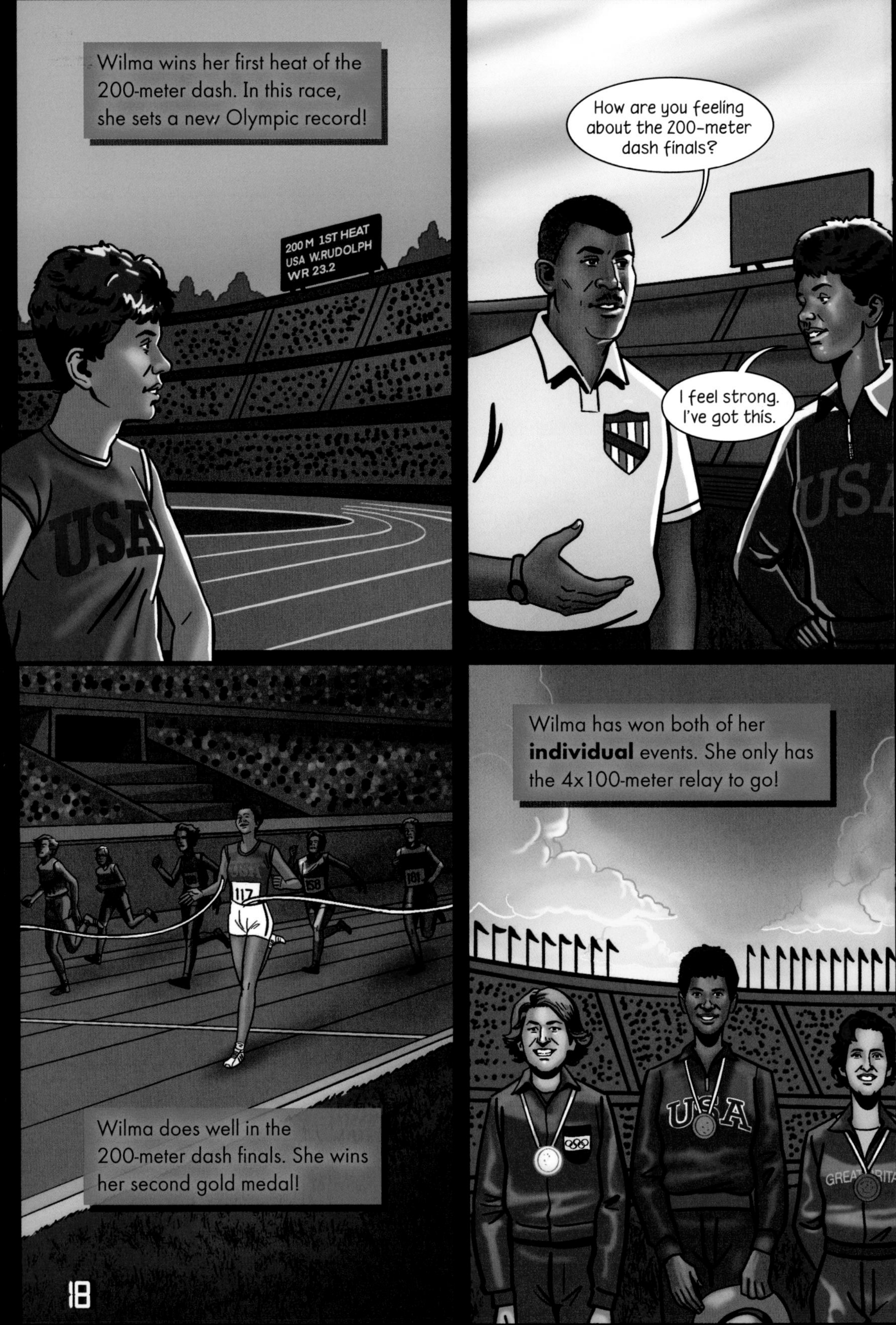
Wilma wins her first heat of the 200-meter dash. In this race, she sets a new Olympic record!
200 M 1ST HEAT
USA W.RUDOLPH
WR 23.2
How are you feeling about the 200-meter dash finals?
I feel strong. I've got this.
Wilma does well in the 200-meter dash finals. She wins her second gold medal!
Wilma has won both of her **individual** events. She only has the 4x100-meter relay to go!

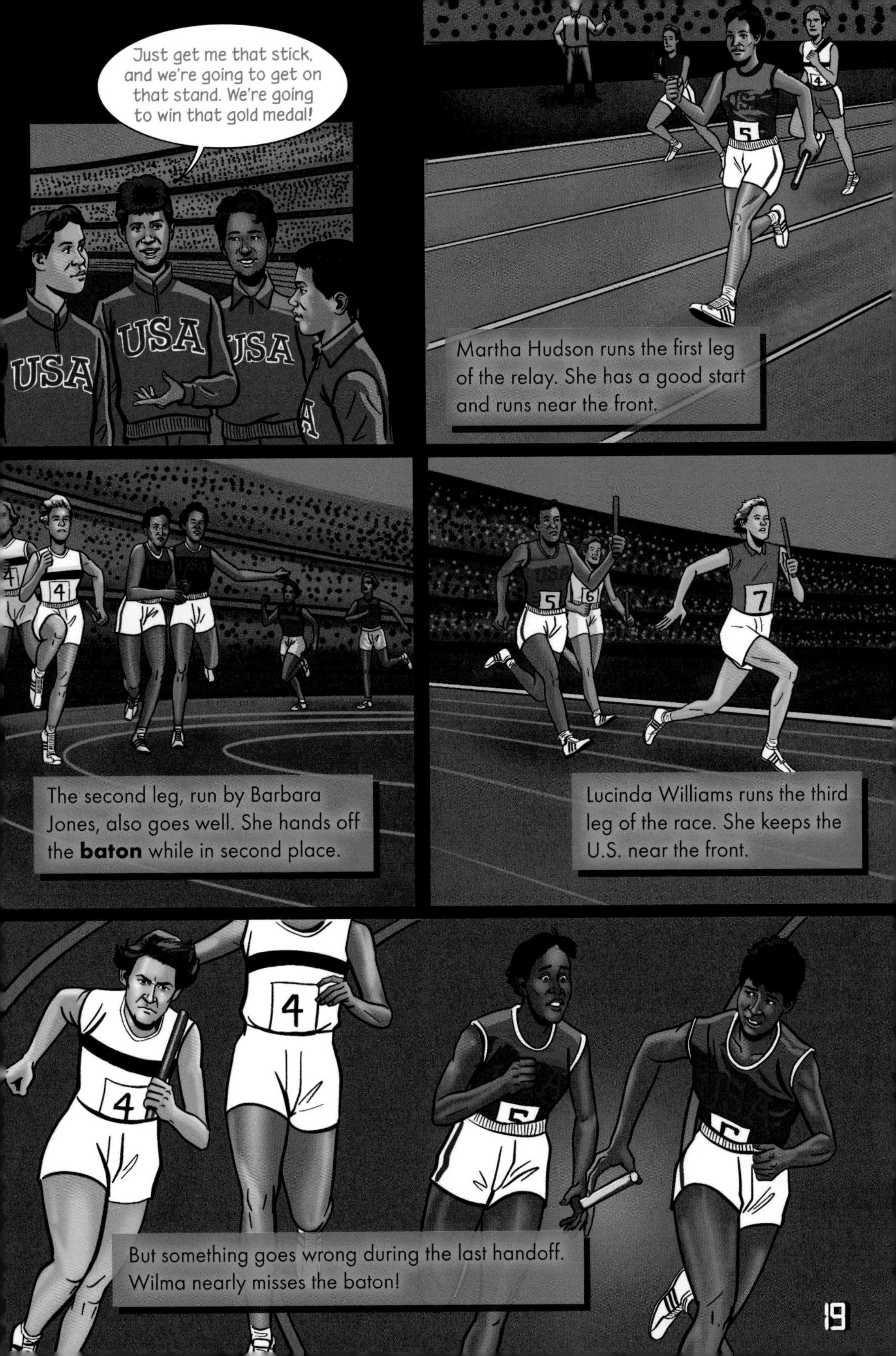

Just get me that stick, and we're going to get on that stand. We're going to win that gold medal!
USA
USA
USA
Martha Hudson runs the first leg of the relay. She has a good start and runs near the front.
The second leg, run by Barbara Jones, also goes well. She hands off the **baton** while in second place.
Lucinda Williams runs the third leg of the race. She keeps the U.S. near the front.
But something goes wrong during the last handoff. Wilma nearly misses the baton!

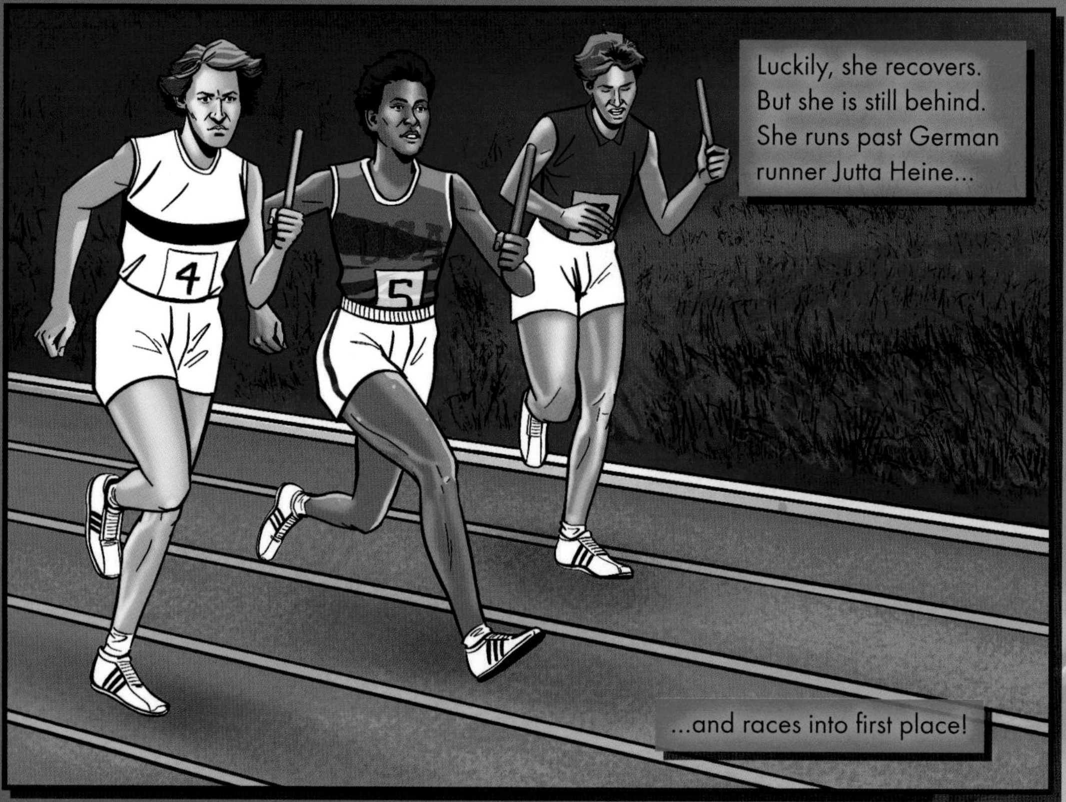
Luckily, she recovers. But she is still behind. She runs past German runner Jutta Heine...
...and races into first place!

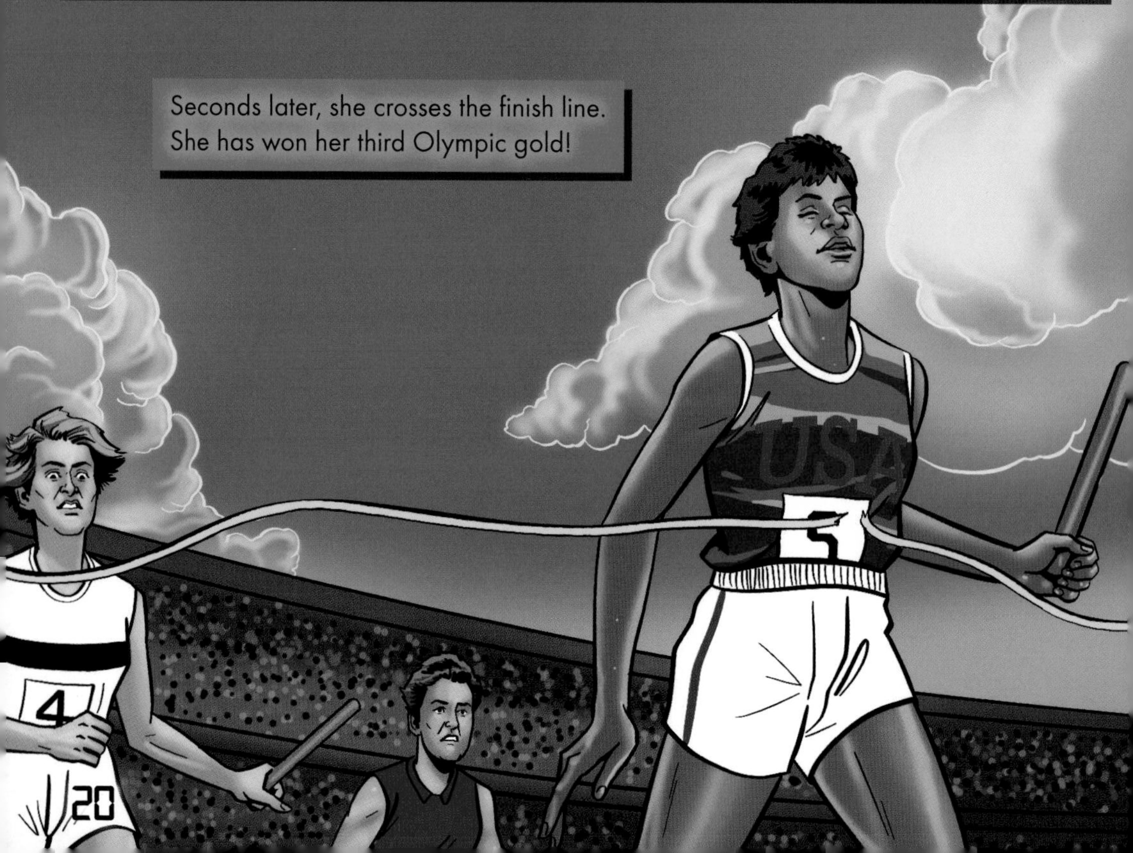
Seconds later, she crosses the finish line. She has won her third Olympic gold!

As a child, doctors said Wilma would never be able to walk without a brace. But she proves them wrong by becoming the first American woman to win three gold medals during the same Olympics!

Wilma's performance makes her a star. When she gets back to the U.S., she goes on tour and gives interviews for several months.

Two years later, Wilma decides to retire from racing. She wins the last race she enters.

Wilma overcame many challenges to become an accomplished Olympian. Her life continues to inspire people today!

MORE ABOUT WILMA RUDOLPH

- When Wilma returned to Tennessee, her hometown held a parade in her honor. It was the town's first public event that was not segregated.

- Wilma was named the Associated Press Female Athlete of the Year in 1960 and 1961.

- A movie about Wilma's life was made in 1977.

- In 1983, Wilma was added to the United States Olympic Hall of Fame.

- After retiring from racing, Wilma became an elementary school teacher.

WILMA RUDOLPH TIMELINE

1940
Wilma is born on June 23

1960
Wilma wins three gold medals during the Summer Olympics in Rome

1994
On November 12, Wilma passes away after a battle with cancer

1956
At the Summer Olympics in Melbourne, Wilma earns a bronze medal

1962
Wilma retires from racing

ROME, ITALY

EUROPE

GLOSSARY

assembly—a gathering of students and teachers to celebrate a person or team

baton—a stick passed from runner to runner in a relay race

endurance—the ability to do something for a long time

heat—an early race in a sporting event

individual—related to an event for one person

leg—one person's part in a relay race

Olympic Trials—competitions held to decide which athletes will compete in each event

paralyzed—unable to move

pneumonia—an illness that affects the lungs

polio—a disease that can make a person unable to move parts of the body

qualify—to be allowed to participate in a certain event

relay—a race between teams of four runners

scarlet fever—an illness that usually leads to a rash, fever, and sore throat

scholarship—money for education that is earned through academic, athletic, or artistic achievement

segregated—separated based on race

tournament—a series of games in which several teams try to win an overall prize

TO LEARN MORE

AT THE LIBRARY

Leed, Percy. *Wilma Rudolph: Running for Gold*. Minneapolis, Minn.: Lerner Publications, 2021.

Rathbun, Betsy. *Rumble in the Jungle: Muhammad Ali vs. George Foreman*. Minneapolis, Minn.: Bellwether Media, 2024.

Rosen, Karen. *Trailblazing Women in Track and Field*. Chicago, Ill.: Norwood House Press, 2023.

ON THE WEB

FACTSURFER

Factsurfer.com gives you a safe, fun way to find more information.

1. Go to www.factsurfer.com
2. Enter "Wilma Rudolph" into the search box and click 🔍.
3. Select your book cover to see a list of related content.

INDEX